*Under
Grandma's Quilt*

By Rho

For information, contact Rho at:
          RHO, PO Box 131875, St. Paul, MN 55113-0021

ISBN: 0-9744552-0-2

Scripture quotations are taken from the *Holy Bible*, New International Version.
© 1973, 1978, 1984 by International Bible Society.
Used by permission of Zondervan Publishing House.

Photography by Anna
Edited by Char/Studio106
Layout by Molly
Proofread by Joni and Joy/Studio106
Cover design by Laura/Studio106

Printed in the United States of America

I was a six-year-old Mrs. Cleaver. You may have seen me walking down the street pushing a buggy full of dolls. My dolls were my babies, so I had many children. I walked with ease and pride—brown curls bouncing, freckles across my nose, and a shy smile. My cupboard was always full as my mom would give me empty food boxes and cans to play with. My pretend husband would come home from work every night to a delicious "meal." I was the Queen of Pretend, and all was perfect in my fairy-tale world.

I was a 24-year-old battered wife. You may have seen me walking down the street pushing a stroller carrying two small children. Only now my walk was slow and timid—black eye, bruises, and a split, swollen lip—there was no smile at all. My children were my only joy. My cupboard was often empty unless I had food stamps. My real-life husband didn't come home for dinner after work because he rarely had a job or because he chose to party with his friends. I was the Queen of Survival, and nothing was easy in my world.

Perhaps I am not any different from you. I know a lot of the same things you may know. I know terror and I know being hunted. I know pain, scars, humiliation, worthlessness, shame, and betrayal. I know feeling alone—convinced that no one could love me. I know guilt, bitterness, retaliation, rage, jealousy. After 19 years of marriage I finally left my husband. That was 13 years ago, and now I know some new things. I know about having a second chance. I know forgiveness, peace, loving, and being loved. I know joy and laughter. I know hope.

And that is why I have written this little book. I want you to find these things too. Most of all, I want you to realize that you are special, you are loved, and you do have hope.

If you are reading this, it may be because you are abused or you care for someone who is. If you are being abused, my first concern is, are you safe? Are your children safe? Do you have a plan of escape in place? At the back of this book are telephone numbers that you can call to obtain help along with some suggestions for a safety plan.

My story is true but I have changed all of the names to fictitious ones for protection. I am sure you understand why.

How it Was

I graduated from high school in the late '60s and from there I went to beauty school while still living at home. When I received my cosmetology license, I was excited but scared. Suddenly I was moving to a slightly larger town an hour away where I had landed a job in a beauty shop. I had never been away from home much, and even when I had gone to church camp as a kid, I would get so lonesome that I would be sent home on day two or three. Now it was time for me to move out on my own.

My family helped me move into my apartment on a Sunday afternoon, and as they drove away my younger sister cried, "It sure is hard to get rid of a sister!" I remember walking up the stairs to my apartment as if I was on death row. This wasn't church camp—this was permanent. The next morning, as I was getting ready for my first day at my new job, there was a knock on my door. It was my dad! He had driven the 75 miles just to take me out for breakfast before work. Mom and Dad knew how lonely and scared I was.

For the first four months, until my roommate joined me, I was one homesick girl. Every night I would walk across the street to the phone booth and call home and cry for my allowed 10 minutes. I'm sure Mom and Dad could hardly wait to get those phone calls!! Each weekend I went home and absorbed all the love and family I could squeeze in. It became easier after my roommate moved in, and a short time later I met Steve.

It was the first part of February in the early '70s when we met. Hemlines were high, hairdos were big, and snowdrifts were deep. My roommate, Sarah, our friend Barb, and I worked in the same beauty shop. We had just gotten off work and were on our way home. Sarah and I had an apartment above the shoe store next to Woolworth's on Main Street, right in the middle of downtown. We were driving down Main and came along side a car with three incredibly cute guys that Barb knew. It wasn't long before we were all cruisin' Main together.

The guys said that they knew about a haunted house outside of town, and so we decided it would be fun to check it out. The house sat at the end of a snow-filled driveway. We all climbed out of the car and in spite of our short skirts, plowed through the snowdrifts while the guys were telling us scary stories. Sarah and one of the guys went up to the house, but I stayed back with the others as my legs were about to freeze off. There was more snow than skirt, and it was cold! The guy who stayed next to me started throwing snowballs through the already broken windows of the house. When the snowballs landed inside, it sounded like someone was in there. The two brave ones who had walked up to the house came running back, screaming, while the rest of us laughed. We scrambled back into the car and left. I ended up sitting next to the snowball thrower. His name was

Steve. He was tall and had incredible brown eyes. He was witty, had us in stitches—and he paid a lot of attention to me.

On our way back into town we drove around a curve and found the road full of pigs that had escaped some farmer's pigpen. Steve grabbed my mittens, got out of the car, and ran after the pigs to clear the road. He got back into the car carrying a very distinct odor, and it didn't take me long to realize my mittens were beyond a good airing out. I told him he owed me a new pair, and that was the beginning of us.

I was in love. We dated until Christmas, and then he proposed. We married the following August. As the wedding drew closer, there were moments when I had second thoughts, but it was never because he was violent. I hadn't seen that side of him yet. It was because we were different in so many ways. Yet Steve had my heart. He could be so boyish, incredibly sexy, and always very funny. And . . . I was sure he had Mr. Cleaver potential!

As time went on, I suspected that my parents didn't care for him. While that was important to me, I also wanted to prove their concerns to be wrong. I occasionally wondered if I was making a mistake but could not bear the thought of hurting his feelings if I broke it off.

Our first year of marriage was just as it should have been—fun and exciting. We bought a mobile home that I fixed up like a doll house. My cooking was atrocious, but our home was cute! Natalie was born 16 months after we said "I do," and Steve adored her. When he came home for lunch, the first thing he did was pick her up and leave dirty hand marks on her sides. As soon as he went back to work, I put clean clothes on her but I didn't mind—I thought it was cute.

Shortly after Natalie was born, Steve's brother-in-law came to see us and introduced Steve to the drums. He became obsessed with playing and caught on to drumming very quickly. In a very short time he was playing with a couple of guys down at one of the local bars. Steve became an overnight sensation with the bar crowd, and it fed something in him. The more he played, the more he wanted stardom and spent most of his time in the bars. He was important there, and his sense of humor added to his appeal. Before long he was drinking more and working less. That was the beginning of the end of us but it dragged on for 17 more years. I tried different things to make him love me more than the gang at the bar but to no avail. And to add further insult to my already injured heart, when the bars closed, Steve found other places to go and other women to be with. I felt utterly rejected and lonely.

At first I cried and begged him to start acting like a married man and a father but he wouldn't—he was having too much fun. By now Tony had made his grand entrance at almost 11 pounds! Tony and Natalie were only 15 months apart so I was a busy mom. But to Steve, the night life had become more important to him. He didn't want to change because he didn't think he was doing anything wrong. He liked his new lifestyle, and our little family seemed an inconvenience to him. Realizing that Steve wasn't going to change to be with me, I made a decision to change to be with him. I started going to the bars and drinking. In the beginning I found excitement in his world. It was so different from the way I had grown up, and I often thought my churchy family didn't know what they were missing out on. Guys actually paid attention to me, and I found a new weapon. Steve had hurt me countless times with other women. Now I could make him jealous so he could see what it was like. If he could see that other men were attracted to me, maybe he would decide he wanted me after all. It was a stupid idea and, of course, it didn't work. It just made him angry. He would accuse me of flirting and being unfaithful. If I disagreed, he beat me because he said that I was lying. If I agreed and said he was right, he would still beat me.

By now I had started playing in the band and the extra money helped us, but the lifestyle was destructive. I felt increasingly empty and knew this was not what I wanted our children subjected to. Other than playing in the band, I stopped hanging out at the bars but Steve continued. While he thrived in this environment, I felt comfortable only when hiding behind my keyboards.

Our life was topsy-turvy. Steve would be out all night and sleep during the day. He would get up just in time to clean up and pick a fight, which always gave him an excuse to storm out of the house and not come back again until early the next morning.

I remember late one afternoon Steve came down into the kitchen. Both of the kids were up from their naps and eating their treat. I was on my hands and knees washing the kitchen floor. Steve was angry because I wouldn't stop what I was doing to make him something to eat so he kicked the pail of soapy water across the floor and water flew all over. Both kids sat in a puddle, crying, with their treat all wet. I ended up lying beside them crying too. Steve was on his way out the door to start another night of partying. He felt justified for leaving because I wouldn't feed him the moment he demanded it.

So many times I thought I couldn't continue this charade and left, but I always came back. I "missed" him, and he always managed to convince me that he would stop beating me, get a real job, leave the bar scene, and be faithful. He would cry, I would feel guilty for hurting him by leaving with the kids, and I would go back to him. Finally one day while sitting in the welfare office, waiting to get food stamps and other help, I looked at my kids and thought, "This is it, I'm not doing this anymore." I picked them up and went home. I put our clothes in laundry baskets so it would look like I was going to the laundromat if Steve happened to catch us. I left a note on the fridge that told him I was leaving and would not consider coming back until he had a job and I saw his first paycheck. I thought if he got a full-time job, he wouldn't have time to run with the guys at the bar and would turn into a responsible and loving father and husband. I was still convinced he could turn into a Mr. Cleaver.

I was a wreck until I got to my parents' house. I was terrified Steve would chase me down and kill me. The violent beatings had been going on for a couple of years now, so I was well acquainted with his anger and how out of control he got.

Steve found a job in another town, I came back home with the kids, and we all moved away from his bar friends. Life started to seem normal. After a time we were able to buy the duplex we lived in, and outward appearances indicated that we were a happy, functioning family. But privately our marriage was one huge festering wound with only a thin scab grown over it to keep everything from spilling out.

> Is there a way to wipe out the sad times—
> The times we've hurt each other?
> The mean things that were said,
> The wrong things that were done,
> If there's a way, I wish you would tell me.
>
> Is there a time when all hurts are gone—
> When we feel healed and joy inside?
> When laughter is always
> And crying is never,
> If there's a time, I wish you would tell me.
>
> Is there a place where we can go—
> Where we can be alone?
> Where our past cannot hurt us
> And the memories don't haunt us.
> If there's a place, I wish you would tell me.
>
> Too many heartaches and too many tears,
> Too many sad times back through the years.
> But tonight when I look at you I know I will stay
> Because each tomorrow must be better
> Than all our yesterdays.

That was my hope. That we could put the past behind and start out fresh. And in some ways it seemed we did. But by now alcohol had a strong hold on Steve, and too much of our past came with us.

The marriage existed for another 13 years after we moved. I can now finally say that there are some good memories from that time but if you were to keep score, the bad memories far outweigh the good. I honestly cannot tell you how many times I left him, but I will tell you about the last two.

It was the Wednesday night before Halloween. Our band had practice at the lodge of a nearby resort, and Steve was in a surly mood from the very beginning of the evening. Nothing was right—I couldn't sing right; I couldn't work my mic right; I couldn't play right. He sat behind the drum set and criticized me nonstop. I finally told him I'd had enough. I was feeling somewhat brave because the band and the resort owner were there. I knew Steve wouldn't get snarly at the moment, but I also knew that I would probably pay for it later. Right in the middle of a song, he went up to the bar for a drink and just sat there. He refused to practice or help tear down when we were done. He was angry. I had gone too far. It was OK for him to humiliate me in front of others, but it was not acceptable for me to do the same to him.

I left and drove home while Steve stayed at the lodge. As I drove down the hill toward our house, I had an overwhelming feeling that I should grab the kids and leave, but I didn't. I can't tell you why I didn't follow my instincts. I knew it was going to be bad. I think that somewhere in the back of my mind was the idea that maybe, just maybe, he would realize how out of line he was. This time he would tell me that I was right, and he was sorry. I still wanted to believe this could happen.

I lay in bed waiting. I heard the car pull into the driveway, the car door close, and footsteps as he walked up the sidewalk. Then I heard the front door open and close, the dog running to greet him, and Steve's footsteps coming up the stairs. He turned on the light, and tore off my blankets. On his face was a look I had never seen before. His usually well-placed slugs had turned into a rage that was totally out of control. With each blow, he screamed, "Slut, whore, baby killer!" He would stop hitting me long enough to pace back and forth at the foot of the bed crying and screaming, "Why do you make me do this to you? Why do you want to keep making me so angry? It isn't my fault that I do this to you; you deserve it! No one else would put up with you! You should be glad that I do because you are nothing but a filthy slut, a whore, a baby killer." And I would think, "You are right, I am worthless. I don't deserve anything better. I am a terrible person. I killed my baby. I am getting what I deserve." Yet this little voice said, "No, he is wrong."

The more he talked, the wilder he got until he was back on top of me punching and screaming. His face was so close to mine that I could feel his spit spraying my face and smell the alcohol on his breath. Inside I screamed, "Please God, he is going to kill me! Stop him, STOP HIM, STOP HIM!" Then he got up and started talking again—and hitting. This cycle went on for several hours. And then he suddenly quit. He lay down on the bed, curled into the fetal position, and waved for me to get out. I climbed out of bed and with my back against the wall, I inched out of the room expecting him to lunge at me. I went downstairs and collapsed. I had to be at work in two hours and I was a mess. I couldn't afford to miss any more work. I knew I had to go. It never occurred to me to call the police. It certainly never occurred to me to see if Steve was OK as he was still lying on the bed upstairs. I thought he may be having a heart attack, and I simply didn't care.

I went to work that morning. The tops of my hands were bruised and badly swollen from trying to ward off the blows. My head hurt from being pummeled and having my hair pulled. My arms and legs were bruised and swollen. My chest was bruised. My lip was split. My face swollen.

That night after work I had a perfect opportunity to escape, but instead I went home. My children were still there. I did not deserve to be happy. I was useless, worthless, very, very homely . . . and alone. So very alone.

I walked in the door that night not sure what to expect. The kids were in the living room with Steve, and he acted as if nothing had happened. He was teasing our now teenage kids—all kindness and fun. I was exhausted and in pain. The kids were watching me closely so I tried to act like everything was fine; they had nothing to worry about. I had just taken off my shoes inside the door when Steve told me in a quiet, soothing voice to put them back on. We were going for a ride; he said we needed to talk. My fear was that he wanted to go parking and have sex. That was often his pattern. I didn't want to go, but I couldn't bear the thought of what he would do to me if I said no.

We climbed into the van, not speaking. I knew this was a bad idea. We drove into town and went to a liquor store. I thought I could take off when he went into the store, but Steve told me to come in. Inside, I cautiously gazed at the exit door and thought maybe I could escape, but I felt paralyzed. We got back into the van, he opened his bottle, and we drove in silence out into the country to an unfamiliar area. I looked at different locations and buildings along the way and thought, "That would be a good place to escape."

As Steve drove around, he reached down beside his seat and picked up a little orange Gideon Bible. "Where in the world did he get that?" I wondered. He handed the Bible to me and said that since I wanted to be such a goody two-shoes like my mommy and daddy, I should look up some verses and read them to him. I had to randomly open the Bible; then he would jab at a verse, and force me to read it in a loud, clear voice. I couldn't believe the way he could take any verse I read and twist it to show how horrible I was as a wife and a person. Outloud I agreed to everything he said I was, but inside there was still this small voice telling me I was not all those horrible things. I looked out the window at the stars, and in my head pleaded, "God, you've got to get me out of here, he's going to kill me tonight."

Steve took the Bible from me and drove home. I was so relieved. I thought I had survived and everything would be OK, but instead, a half mile from our house, he pulled into a field. I thought, "Oh no, now he wants sex." He turned off the van and we sat there, in the dark, in the middle of this field where I could see the yard lights of the neighbors next to our house. Home was so close, yet I was in another world. We sat in silence. I waited. In the quiet, he calmly said, "There's going to be a murder-suicide in this field tonight." He held up a brick and asked if I wanted to feel it against my skull a little at a time or all at once, full force. The beating began—more violent than the night before. His rage was indescribable. His hatred toward me was fierce. Then it stopped. As quickly as it started, it stopped. I was confused and more frightened than I had ever been. He turned on the engine, backed out of the field, and drove the short distance home. Without a word, he parked the van and walked over to the bar at the resort next to our home. I found my broken glasses on the floor and, in great pain, slowly crawled out of the van and stumbled into the house. I pleaded with the kids to come with me but Tony wouldn't. Within 10 minutes, Natalie and I left, backing my car out of the driveway, headlights off, to sneak away to my sister's. I knew he wouldn't find his way there. I had survived another beating but I was sure the next one would be fatal. I couldn't be there when he got home from the bar that night because I could not withstand another attack.

The next morning I called him. Yes, I called him. I was worried about Tony and I didn't want Steve to be mad that I had left. I needed to know that he understood why, which of course now I know was an impossible wish. That night our band was to play for the Halloween dance. He told me I was letting the whole band down if I didn't show. He blamed me for driving him so crazy. It was my fault if our family broke up. It was my fault if our band broke up. I shouldn't push him so far.

I went back.

I played with the band for the Halloween dance. It was a long, long night. I was in so much pain and utterly exhausted. Steve was gentle and caring. While I didn't trust him, I was too tired and worn to resist it. I welcomed the quietness and comfort because I needed it.

The next week was the typical "honeymoon" part of the violence cycle. Maybe you've heard of it—the buildup (tension), release (beating), honeymoon (comforting and false promises). It was a relief to my battered mind and body. Although this had been going on for many years, there was a part of me that, in spite of everything, hoped this would be the last time. In what seemed like an odd answer to prayer, Steve told me the beatings had to stop as they were too hard on his body. He couldn't handle it anymore, and I ended up comforting him. Never mind how awfully beaten and bruised I was. It was all so twisted.

A week later, Steve went over to the resort next door to play euchre with the Saturday morning gang. I stayed home to clean and enjoy the early morning lake; how I loved it. Steve came home around 11 a.m. looking for something to eat. He became furious when he saw something that was not put away properly in the refrigerator. He started screaming that I was lazy and hit me repeatedly on the back of the head. He told me to pack my bags and get out. I ran upstairs and threw some clothes into a bag. In moments I was coming down the steps when Steve met me at the bottom and dragged me back upstairs into the bathroom. He shoved my face against the window screen and began choking me. His fingers were growing tighter and tighter around my neck until my son and a friend intervened and pulled him off. I told Steve this was the end. I was filing for a divorce on Monday.

I didn't file. He left for Arizona the next day to "cool down." His intent was to live with his brother, but I feared it would not last very long. I called him often during the three weeks he was there. It wasn't because I wanted to work things out. It was because I knew I would be safe for at least another 23 hours. It would take him that long to drive home. The last time I talked to him he said he was coming home, and I told him that when he did, I would be gone. He was infuriated. I knew well enough what he would do to me when he got home, and this time I was determined to not be there.

But my children didn't feel that way. They wouldn't leave with me. It was as if they had forgotten all the things that had happened before Steve left. I begged them to come with me but they wouldn't. They were 15 and 16 years old, and I couldn't pick them up and carry them to the car. They were already bigger than I. They didn't seem to be afraid of him. Yet they reminded me of the ugly things Steve had said if I ever took them away from him again. I had to make a choice between life and being with my children.

I left alone.

I was frantic and left for a battered women's shelter. I borrowed $20 from a friend to put gas in our rickety old van and set out on that slippery, cold winter night and drove to a town about 1½ hours away. It was a place where I knew Steve would never find me.

It was very hard to stay away. My determination and courage didn't last long, and I desperately missed my children. When I called, Steve rarely let me talk to them. This was his way of punishing me for leaving. The conversations with the kids were strained and when they told me that his mood worsened after we talked, I felt that for their safety, it was better to call less frequently.

Soon I was calling Steve trying to say all the right things. I needed him to understand me and why I left so that I could talk to my children. He wanted me home one minute, he threatened to move the kids to Arizona the next. He loved me, he hated me. He screamed, then he would cry. It was all so confusing. When I would hear the voice of the sweet, funny man I had fallen in love with, it dulled my mind. I didn't hear the voice of the violent man he could turn into. Always the responsible one, I was convinced that Steve needed me to take care of him and, furthermore, it was up to me to make this family work. I needed to be with my children, and I needed Steve to love me like he once did long ago. I needed to know that I was worth changing for. I was lonely, and I wanted to believe that he would never hit me again.

I moved back.

This time Steve had actually told the truth. He didn't hit me after that; the physical violence turned into something much different. He often drove me to work. Sometimes he would pull into the parking lot to drop me off and then suddenly back out and take me to the nearest convenience store and force me to call in sick. He would tell me that we needed this time together, and we'd go parking or go home and watch disgusting videos and spend the day in bed.

When the kids came home from school, he would go off to the bar. I could always expect him home around 1 a.m. As before, I heard his footsteps coming up the sidewalk, heard the door open, and heard him coming up the steps—always expecting the worst. Sometimes he would just drop into bed and fall asleep, but more often he would lie very quietly while I pretended to be asleep. I could always tell by his breathing that he was still awake. Then . . . bam . . . Steve would reach over, yank off my blankets, and say, "Talk to me." It didn't matter whether or not I said anything, his rage grew on nothing. He paced back and forth at the foot of the bed berating me for everything I ever did and ever was and ever would be. He did not beat me with his fists or feet anymore, he beat me with his voice. He could go on for hours. He came close to me screaming obscenities, spraying my face with his spit. I could smell the alcohol and the smoke on his breath. It was the same pattern as the physical beatings, but all launched by the three words "Talk to me."

Some nights before he got home, I would try to think up things that I could say that would be believable. Occasionally they worked but never more than once. I would tell him I was worried about money; I had a bad day at work; I wished I wasn't so fat; someone said something to me that was hurtful. He was quick to counter them with "Are you saying I am lazy because I don't work?" Or, "Quit trying to make your job sound so important. You're too stupid to have an important job." Or, "You are a disgusting pig. If it bothers you so much, change it. I can't do everything." Or, "You probably deserved having something mean said to you. See, no one else can put up with you either." It got to where I was better off saying nothing at all. To this day, when someone says, "Talk to me," I freeze.

The night that I finally left Steve for the last time was in July 1991. After the horrors endured in our marriage, it was a simple five dollar bill that was the last straw—the same thing that started the first of countless beatings. Steve wanted to go out, and I said we had no money. He asked our daughter if he could borrow 5 dollars. I told him that if we were going to stoop to borrowing money from our daughter, the money should go for milk and bread and not be spent at the bar. He stormed out of the house screaming threats. I knew the anger had been building for a very long time; I knew that he was close to exploding. The kids went to bed, and I paced the floor. I was so afraid. I would look out the windows at the stars and ask God to please show me what to do. When Steve came home, he was drunk and mean. I told him I was done. This time it was for good. It took me 19 years to realize that it was never going to change. Our marriage was not held together by love; it was held together by fear.

He just looked at me and laughed, but the scar on his chin quivered so I knew he was angry. He told me to get out but leave my wedding ring on the hutch. I left with a sleeping bag and a little suitcase that held a few clothes, some toiletries, and my needlepoint. I walked down the stairs into the living room, and he laughed some more. He thought I was being dramatic and foolish. I had nowhere to go, no way to get there, and no money. I knew if I admitted defeat this time, it might literally be the last nail in my coffin.

Once again, I pleaded with the kids to please come with me, and once again they said, "No." They were now 16 and 17. They firmly said they would not leave the house. Thinking back, I do not think it was a parent choice although it certainly felt that way. It was a home choice. Plus, I was leaving at 2 a.m. with no idea of where I was going or how I was going to get there.

I left alone.

Our home was on a lake next to a resort. On the opposite side of the resort is a long dirt road that is lined with lake cabins on one side and a steep, wooded hill on the other side. Because Steve would not allow me to take a car, I walked down that dark, desolate cabin road, hoping his sister and family would be at their cabin. I was aware of every sound and expected Steve to lunge from behind a tree and beat me in the way he told me he would if I ever left him again.

His sister let me stay at their cabin the rest of the night and then brought me to work the next day. I had no money, and I had no idea where I was going to go that night. My boss took money from his personal savings account for me to live on until I was paid. I was afraid to stay with family or friends as I knew I was endangering them because of Steve's wrath. I stayed in a crummy motel for three weeks and then rented a two-bedroom apartment. The landlord let me split the damage deposit into several payments. My sister helped me "move in." I had a sleeping bag, a small suitcase, a few more clothes (my mom lent me some), and a tiny black-and-white TV that I bought at a garage sale for $10 along with a lamp I bought for $2. We each took one trip with our arms full and I was fully moved in! Later family and friends brought me dishes, linens, hangers, toiletries, and some furniture. Nothing matched and everything was used, but it was the most beautiful apartment in the world.

My children still would not come and live with me. Again Steve punished me by hanging up when I called to talk to the kids. However, he never hesitated to call me and tell me I had better get some heating fuel delivered to the house, or that the kids needed money for school lunches or pictures. I'd better help pay the mortgage, pay medical or phone bills, or drop off groceries. Because it was for my children, I did what he demanded until I was advised by Social Services to stop. Because it was not court ordered, the court would not consider this when looking at back child support. The kids needed to realize they could not have these things as long as they remained with their unemployed father.

It seemed heartless and cruel. I had to get them out of that house. I was afraid Steve's rage would spill over to them. He called me at all hours of the night, threatening to burn down my apartment or come and get me if I hung up on him. He told me to call the police because he was on his way. He harassed me in the parking lot of my workplace. He was beyond reasoning and was agitated and frantic. What was he doing with my kids? Was his behavior toward them just as unreasonable? His persistence was frightening.

And then he suddenly changed. He let the kids visit me. He was kinder on the phone and actually seemed concerned with how I was doing. It felt like a trap but I didn't want to challenge it because I was seeing the kids more often. I let my guard down. One night he came to pick up the kids', and I made the mistake of letting Steve inside. At first he was gentle and very funny but that didn't last long. He carried on for three hours about how we should be a family and how I should stop destroying it. I was wearing down. I could hardly bear to be apart from the kids any longer. I was so close to giving in. Through eyes filled with tears, I looked at Tony sitting on the floor. He looked up and mouthed to me, "Don't give in, Mom." He knew. With his young years, he had painful wisdom. As they left, Steve blasted me with more threats. I knew I could never be alone with him again. The next day I filed an Order for Protection.

Then I called Child Protection. I needed to get the kids out of that house, but it had to look like it was not their idea so their father could not hold it against them. Child Protection could do nothing unless there was a "recent occurrence." Unbelievable! Before they could react, one of my children would have to be hurt first—whatever happened to being proactive?

I called the high school principal. All of this was having an effect on them in school. Was there a way the school could intercede and require counseling for them? Tony was filled with anger, and Natalie was in denial and shutting down. Their principal couldn't do anything but promised to monitor them closely.

WHAT COULD I DO? I felt helpless. Had I done the right thing? Was I selfish in leaving them? I would pace my apartment at all hours of the night, clutching their pictures to my heart, sobbing with a physical pain that was too much to bare. I had left my children with the man who tried to kill me twice. What kind of a mother was I? But had I stayed, I would have been a dead mother. I cried, "Please, dear God, only you have the power to rescue my children from this. Please, please hear me!"

I never went back.

My marriage had ended, and my life as I had known it was over. Steve honored the Order for Protection but it was hard to trust that piece of paper. I slept with a hammer beside me and my window open so I could hear noises outside. Each time I came home I inspected my apartment with a screwdriver to make sure he wasn't hiding somewhere. Nearly every night was filled with sobs of anguish for my children and their safety. But I did it. I found a courage and strength that hadn't been destroyed after all. We all have it. No matter how bad you have been beaten down, somewhere in there is that will. Dig down, my friend. It is there.

The tree stood alone in the empty yard
With hidden strength though scarred from the past.
Against hard rains and heavy snow it had fought hard;
By its Creator's strength it knew it would last.

The constant winds caused branches to break
And slowly the tree was splitting apart
Yet leaving a strong foundation with which to make
A new beginning, a brand-new start.

The new branches slowly spread out and reached beyond
Where the old branches had ended.
New buds unfolded to leaves and beauty was found
After the tree, by its Creator, had mended.

And now when a constant wind comes along,
The tree knows its time has not come to an end.
Though branches may break and fall to the ground
It knows with time, it will always mend.

I lost my job in December and on that same day, I was served with child support papers. It seemed that the more I prayed, the worse things became. Maybe I was the terrible person Steve always told me I was. I could not understand it. In December and January I was at the lowest time in my life. I hid in my apartment for days at a time. If I had to go to the employment office or to my part-time job, I was filled with anxiety and started getting ready hours before I had to be there because I was afraid I would be late and get into trouble. At the end of January, I was told that Steve lost the house and soon the kids would be with me. That gave me the jolt I needed. I could hardly wait to have them back.

It was eight months after I left Steve when my kids came home to me. I remember that moment as if it was yesterday. I was at the kitchen sink washing dishes when they knocked on the door. They looked like my little children even though they towered over me. They were very quiet and walked in slowly. I gave them each an unreturned hug. They had no emotion. I knew I had to give them time. They had been through too much. I wanted to stay close to them and it was hard for me to not constantly touch them. They needed to learn what it was like to be safe. I didn't want to put them on the defense. I made some mistakes, but it didn't take long before we were talking easier and laughing too. We rarely talked about the past eight months.

I often look back to that time to remind myself that God had a plan even though everything seemed like a mess. Let me put it in sequential order for you so you can see His plan too. July—I left Steve—alone. August—moved into my apartment. October—started a part-time job so was now working 1½ jobs. November—severely sprained my ankle so I could not work the part-time job. December—lost my full-time job. January—ankle healed and I am back to my part-time job. February—the kids came home to me! March—I got a new full-time job. It was as if God slowly took everything away so that he could give it back to me as I was ready—stronger and healthier in my heart, in my mind, and most of all, in my faith.

It was nine years after I left Steve, when I thought my life was going so well, the three words "talk to me" came back to haunt my dreams. This triggered an avalanche that took almost a year to dig out of. It is that year I want to tell you about.

It began when my daughter and I returned home from spending a few wonderful days on Mackinac Island. I loved spending time with her and realized how much I hated coming home to a too-quiet apartment again. I was tired of being alone. I wanted the companionship of someone. Someone to come home to. The thought came to me that maybe I was finally ready to start meeting men and eventually marry again. The mere thought triggered nightmares. The nightmares triggered memories, the memories triggered anxiety, and then depression. The downward spiral was out of control and I knew I needed to get professional help. I was later diagnosed as having post-traumatic stress disorder.

The same nightmare was constant. In my sleep I could actually feel Steve get into my bed and I could smell the smoke and alcohol. He would jerk off my blankets and say "talk to me." I would wake up in a cold sweat, trembling uncontrollably and could still smell the smoke and alcohol. I'd go into the living room and I could smell it in there too. (My psychologist later told me that smells often trigger memories but when memories trigger smells, that indicates deep trauma.) It would take me a while to settle down, and it got to where I was almost afraid to sleep at all. The hardest part of it, though, was that I started remembering other things that happened in the marriage.

I could find very little that gave me comfort. That's when I thought about the quilt that my grandma had given us as a wedding gift.

> I pulled the quilt from a cardboard box
> Where it was stored for many years.
> It felt cool and soft against my cheek.
> Now, Under Grandma's Quilt, I would face my fears.
>
> The quilt was made by Grandma's worn, gentle hands
> To keep me warm when nights were cold.
> But now it would hold me both day and night
> As my lost memories began to unfold.
>
> The old, tattered quilt had seen better days.
> It was torn; the edges were frayed.
> It seemed to reflect how I felt about myself
> As it caught my tears while I journaled and prayed.
>
> I moved through that time with fear and anger
> My heart filled with sorrow and guilt.
> But with God, I left that all behind
> And found hope Under Grandma's Quilt.

Often, when we go through something like this, we feel vulnerable and exposed. Fear, rejection, and hurt feelings return. We know we are safe but we don't feel that we are. What could represent safety to you? Could it be a quilt or maybe a stuffed toy? Find that symbol of safety and wrap yourself up in it or hold it tightly to your heart. It may sound a bit corny but—it works!

Time to Heal
My Journal

October 31

He saw me sitting there
Trying to look brave
But pressing back against my chair—
Fight hard, fight to save.

I tried to be happy,
Yet so afraid to share.
But he saw through me—
Fight hard, fight to care.

I tried to be strong,
No one can hurt me.
But somewhere things went wrong—
Fight hard, fight to believe.

I'm tired of crying,
I've hated each tear.
And I'm tired of trying—
Fight harder, fight to hear.

Today I had my first visit with my Christian psychologist, Dane. I can't tell you how many times I wanted to cancel. We talked about what brought me to him and immediately tears fell. I hate that I cry so easily. Maybe I will know I am fully healed when I can get through a full session and still have my eye makeup on my eyes and not running off my chin.

I told Dane about my dream and the memories it triggers. Why, after nine plus years is this happening? Did I have a stroke or something? Where have these memories been? The mind is an incredible thing. It can take a "time-out" while we live in our crisis. When I realized I was safe and strong enough to deal with everything, my mind let the memories leak out. Denial for a long period of time can be exhausting and harmful, so while these flashbacks were very hard for me they were also a healthy thing.

He said if I was comfortable, he would like to hear the memories. Of course I am not comfortable! There is nothing in this whole mess that is comfortable. That's why I am here. Help me! I want to be healed. I want to be free of this shadow and of the fear. I want to be healthy in my heart. How quickly can this be done? I want it now!

When I told Dane that I felt terribly weak, he said I was not at all weak because I worked very hard to create this blanket of protection. I have good kids who are doing well, my family is healthy, I have a nice apartment, a nice car, a good job, and great friends. I like my church. But every once in a while something pokes a hole through my security blanket; it frightens me so I hurry and patch my guarded world and life goes on. I can either continue to patch up my life, or I can find out how to prevent the unraveling from happening again. He said it would be hard—very painful—but I knew that nothing could be as painful as the marriage.

After I told him a brief piece of my story, he asked if I had told my whole story to anyone. No, I hadn't. I share a bit here, a bit there and then I hide. He said I needed someone to share the whole story with. I guess he means him, but it's too hard for me to trust anyone at that level. It's too hard to be vulnerable to anyone. The man I wanted to trust ripped me to shreds both verbally and physically in my marriage. That is a hard thing to forget.

About this time I had also started going to a Bible study because I was searching for answers. I had no idea at the time that the Bible study was going to equip me—to make me stronger for what was ahead. 2 Chronicles 16:9a says *"For the eyes of the Lord range throughout the earth to strengthen those whose hearts are fully committed to him . . ."* I feel so alone and yet I know as I sift through all of this I will ultimately be OK. I know God isn't going anywhere.

But tonight all I want to do is hide. I don't want to talk. I don't want to pay bills or do any of the necessary things. I feel so fragile. God, I know you can hear me. I just wish I could feel you comfort me.

November 1

I have been so afraid in the past, and I'm afraid now. The thought of reliving all that horror is too much. I cannot do it. I cannot do this alone. God, do you hear me? I cannot do this alone. I feel as if I have to constantly remind myself that God is with me. For so long I have thought I could depend on no one but myself. Psalm 34:18 says *"The Lord is close to the brokenhearted and saves those who are crushed in spirit."* Oh, God . . . that would be me.

Do you feel alone in this? Do you feel no one would understand? Do you feel you would be disloyal to your abuser if you told anyone about what is happening? Are you embarrassed or ashamed? Do you feel you deserve this abuse? Tell God about it on this journal page.

For I am the Lord, your God, who takes hold of your right hand and says to you, Do not fear; I will help you. (Isaiah 41:13)

November 14

Today I saw Dane. I wondered what we would talk about. It didn't surprise him when I told him that I'd often thought of canceling. We talked about need. I feel needed by so many, but why do I feel my needing is a weakness? For me, it could lead to vulnerability and putting myself in the position of being hurt or disappointed. As a child, I was the oldest and felt responsible for the others. We moved a lot, and I never really locked into friendships with many kids. I was shy, so it was more comfortable for me to stay at home and hide. I still struggle with wanting to hide.

Dane said I am amazingly good at "shifting." I shift the focus from his questions and move to a place that is more comfortable. He asked when it would be my turn to be cared for. It's hard for me. I would rather be perceived as a tough, I-survived-kind-of person. Only those closest to me see my heart. Most everyone else just sees my humor.

We talked about my dreams. He told me that as hard as it is for me to believe this, I need to dream. It's a release. Things build up during the day, and then the subconscious releases the fear and anger at night. The dreams may frighten me, but they can't hurt me. Dane told me that while we talked about my past, the dreams would occur more often for a while.

So now I want to think about this. Why is it OK to be needed but not OK to need? Why do I feel shame for being needy?

Is it hard for you to reach out to others? Is it shameful for you to express a need. God will not laugh at your vulnerability. He will not mock you. He will not use it as an excuse to hurt you. He cares. Tell Him.

For he has not despised or disdained the suffering of the afflicted one; he has not hidden his face from him but has listened to his cry for help. (Psalm 22:24)

November 17

I had another nightmare. Steve and I are outside the van, and he is screaming at me. He's hitting and kicking me in the stomach and chest. I yell at the kids to run and get away. He keeps kicking me. I run. I grab Natalie and carry her—running to catch up with Tony. He keeps getting smaller and smaller. Tony is lying flat like a cookie on a cookie sheet on a conveyor that's moving away from me. I reach out and grab him but I grab him and another little boy. Is this other boy the baby I aborted? I'm so scared because I can still hear Steve's feet pounding behind me as I run away. I wake up and still hear his feet pounding behind me, but then I realize it is my heart pounding instead.

In another dream I'm in a large meadow with trees all around. I am happy and so I want to fly. I take one sweep across the meadow. It feels so good. I take another sweep and suddenly there are cables across the sky and each time I sweep, they get lower and lower, and soon these big, thick cables are pressing me down on the ground. I can't move. Just a short distance away is a little hill. If I can move to that little hill, I can roll down it and then the cables won't be pushing so hard on me, but there is a big, black box or something blocking the way. I'm trapped.

November 19

Sometimes it's nearly impossible for me to feel upbeat, but I put on a show when I'm around the kids. I don't want them to know the hell that's in my mind right now. It's easier on me to hide from people because they are used to me being full of fun, but right now I have no joy. I need restful sleep—not nights full of horror—not days full of terrible memories.

November 26

I have been without nightmares for a couple of nights. It's wonderful. Prayers are being answered. I would like to stop seeing Dane; maybe this is the end. Yet, as easy as it would be for me to walk away, somehow I don't think this is over. I need to deal with the crud that's been stirred up. I'm so grateful for my sisters and my Bible study ladies.

What I have sensed is this: My heart is thawing. It was always there but frozen. Now I feel so tender-hearted.

Do you cry? Have you locked up those tears inside of you? Why? What would happen if you let yourself cry? Do you feel like you would never be able to stop? Would your tears melt the mask you wear? Tell Jesus about it.

Those who sow in tears will reap with songs of joy. He who goes out weeping, carrying seed to sow, will return with songs of joy, carrying sheaves with him. (Psalm 126:5-6)

November 28

Today, I saw Dane. I was so nervous before seeing him that by the time I got into his office incredible anxiety had overtaken me. I'm always worried what we are going to talk about.

He asked if I had any thoughts from our last session. I told him, "I cry so easily right now." What triggers the tears? I wish I knew. It could be anything. It could be nothing. He asked when I quit crying. What happened that made me think crying is bad or weak or wrong? I can't talk about the abortion yet. He thinks my tears are tender. I told him I am tired of crying. "Tears are bad?" he asked. "Yes, I look weak and fragile," I replied.

I asked Dane again, "Why am I going through all of this therapy?" He told me about his son tearing a big hole in his knee. He had to take him to the doctor because it wouldn't heal. The doctor opened the hole and slowly picked out all of the particles that would cause infection or keep it from healing. That's what we are doing in these sessions—slowly cleaning out the wound so it can finally heal.

December 3

He hurt me, and I let him;
It was so many years ago.
I tucked those memories deep in myself,
Now remembering tears at me so.

He beat me, and I let him.
The rage inside me refuses to dim;
It's blinding my frightened soul.
What if I turn into him?

He betrayed me, and I let him.
Will my face ever be dry?
How do the tears from my heart
Find their way to my eyes?

He raped me, and I let him.
Why did I think I deserved no less?
My heart, my mind, my body, my life—
Too afraid to say no but never said yes.

He shamed me, and I let him.
I made my baby die
To save a marriage that had no breath,
Still trying to live a lie.

He hurt me, and I let him,
So I left my heart behind.
But now it's catching up to me—
It keeps crashing into my mind.

Several months later, while going through my journal, I read this poem again. What shattered me was not so much what he did to me but that I still felt I let him. I was taking the blame for all that happened to me. As long as I continued blaming myself, I would continue to punish myself in some way or allow others to do it for me. It was time to stop.

December 16

My visit with Dane left me empty. At one point he leaned forward and said, "Tell me about the beatings." I said, "I don't understand what you mean." How could I explain all the beatings and the surrounding circumstances in 45 minutes? I didn't like it that he leaned into me. I felt pressured and claustrophobic. He was moving into my space. I told him that I didn't want to tell him everything. Yet, I knew I needed to in order to get through this darkness so healing could begin. I told him about the first time I was beaten.

It happened in our bedroom right after Natalie was born and I had just finished feeding her. Steve was angry because he wanted to go out, and I told him we had no money. He immediately became furious. I had never seen him like that. He started hitting me on the head while Natalie lay on the bed screaming. I started to pass out and he told me, "You had better not or I will do something even worse!" When he finished the beating, he left the house. I scooped Natalie up and held her while I lay on the bed sobbing. She must have been so frightened. I didn't understand what had just happened. Hours later he came home full of remorse. He was incredibly tender and loving, and I honestly believed it would never happen again. But of course, it did.

The next beating I remembered was when I was pregnant with Tony and holding Natalie. He kept hitting me on the side of my large, pregnant stomach. I begged him to let me put Natalie down so I wouldn't drop her. When he was done with me, he slammed his hand through the window as he pushed the door open. The broken glass cut his hand; he was bleeding, but I didn't care. I just didn't care. There was so much more I could tell Dane but I couldn't yet. To expose my weaknesses, by telling what really happened, makes me more vulnerable.

That is why I keep people at arm's length. I will be vulnerable to no one. No one can hurt me again. I detest weakness in myself but have compassion toward others because I understand it. So, why don't I feel compassion toward myself? I want to be normal. I want to love again and be loved. How do you learn to trust?

December 28

I met with Dane today. I wanted to talk to him about my anxiety attack on Monday. My sister was with me in my parents' bedroom while I pulled myself together. She was trying to comfort me. I told her I can't handle people being nice to me when I'm like this, so please be mean. Dane interjected "so please beat me up." I stopped cold. That's what it is. I understand beatings. I feel uncomfortable with being comforted.

He won't give me anything for the attacks at this point. He doesn't want them masked. What did I learn about myself? I am not super woman, super daughter, super mom, super sister, super aunt. I am me. I need to cut myself some slack.

January 9

I saw Dane, and right now I question if I'll go back. This is how I feel. My life is like two rocks. One rock is my past—one rock is my present. Both rocks have some smooth places. Both rocks have some rough, jagged edges. Dane takes these two rocks, slams them together, and rubs them back and forth against each other. Sometimes the smooth parts touch and there is peace, but more often, a jagged piece rubs against another jagged piece and parts chip away or maybe a jagged piece hits a smooth part and gouges it. Then I leave his office bleeding, and I have to move the rocks around so they fit—smooth on smooth. If he thinks all of the jagged pieces will soon smooth out, he is full of crap. If he thinks that my childhood has anything to do with why I ended up in a violent marriage, he is a fool.

I'm sick of feeling like a victim every time I leave Dane's office. I try too hard to make my life work and then that jerk drags me through this crap for 45 minutes and I pay him $110. Who's the idiot here?

January 23

Today, I saw Dane. Yes, I had settled down. I was no longer angry with him.

It amazes me that after four months it's still so hard for me to sit in the waiting room. By the time he comes to get me, I'm ready to jump out of my skin, and as soon as I get in his office the tears come. I always wonder what we're going to talk about, and it terrifies me. It finally occurred to me that it was similar to waiting in bed for Steve to come home and wondering what he would want to talk about. I am going to Dane to talk to him, and while he never says "talk to me," that is exactly why I'm there. Dane assured me that we would talk only about what I wanted to. If it was too uncomfortable, just say the word. He said that I have been forced to do things I didn't want to for too long. He wouldn't push me as our relationship is based on trust and comfort. No force.

We talked a little about my childhood and then moved into my marriage. With Steve, I never measured up. He wanted me to be smarter, prettier, skinnier, a better lover, a better cook, use better hygiene, be a partier. "Don't be such a goody two-shoes," he liked to say. Steve could always counter my successes. If I lost weight, I was cheating on him. If I gained weight, I didn't think it was important enough to look nice for him. If I got a promotion, he could not understand why I was so smart at work and so dumb at home. If I didn't want to go to parties, he would find someone who would. If I went to parties, I was babysitting him. He would go days without a shower, yet it was me that was accused of having poor hygiene. No matter what, it was never quite right. I always felt like a failure. I failed people who said they loved me. That is why it's OK for me to love them but not OK for them to love me. If they love me, I will undoubtedly fail them and what would the consequences be?

February 1

David was in our band. He was very talented, I loved to sing with him, and he was very handsome. My friendship with David was important to me. He always told me that I looked pretty or I played well. He would call me at work just to see how my day was going. In my lonely heart, I thought about what it would be like to have an affair with him, but I knew I wouldn't. While I could try and justify that sort of behavior because of how Steve treated me, the fact was that the consequences would never be worth it.

One night Steve came home from the bar, woke me up, woke up the kids, and screamed that I was a slut and a whore. He told me to call David and tell him it was over. What was over? Steve had decided we were having an affair. He forced me to call David at 2 a.m. I said exactly what Steve told me to while my kids stood there listening. David was dumbfounded, but he heard Steve screaming in the background so he figured it out. After I hung up, Steve kept yelling, "You're a whore!" then took me up to the bedroom and staked his claim on my body.

Not too long after, Steve and I were getting ready to go out. He was in a good mood . . . he was always jazzed when we were going to go out. I was standing in front of the mirror combing my hair. Steve came into the bathroom and screamed, "Why can't you wear your hair better? Why can't you wear it more like Donna or Jill? Why do you make yourself even uglier?" He grabbed my brush and combed my hair. It looked ludicrous. It was all brushed over to one side—flat against my head. It looked like a very small helmet on a very large head! I had never seen Jill's or Donna's or anyone else's hair styled that way. I told him I wasn't going anywhere with my hair pasted to my head. He told me that if I was any kind of wife, I would wear my hair for my husband and not other guys. So I went out with my hair the way he'd combed it—plastered into a helmet-do. People kept looking at me. They were obviously staring directly at my hair, and I was completely miserable. As it turned out, Steve paid no attention to me anyway but was busy charming all the other women. There I sat. What a fool.

February 4

Why do I continue dreaming that we are back together? In my dream I am so surprised and I can't remember how it happened but there we are. We are usually living in the duplex but occasionally it is in the house by the lake. I'm frustrated because we are back together. He isn't mean or violent anymore, but I still don't want to be with him. I try to make the best of it but am always wondering how I will get away.

February 5

I saw a lady come to pick up her husband from work tonight. I remembered something. Once a week I had to go to Steve's workplace and step on the scale to see how much weight I had lost or gained. The scale was in the warehouse so it was surrounded by men. The digital read-out was large so everyone could see it. Every week I got into the car, full of dread, and drove out there. I'd wait for his ridicule in front of the guys and his wrath when he got home. If I didn't weigh in, Steve's wrath was twice as bad. What was wrong with me?

Yesterday I saw Dane. I told him that I struggle with feeling like a fool for having stayed in the marriage so long. I told him that I dream Steve and I are back together again, and I am always upset and confused as to how this happened. In my dreams, I wonder how I can get away this time. I feel trapped. What do these ongoing dreams mean? Do they mean that I want us to get back together? How could that possibly be? He said no, it does not mean that at all. Even though we are physically apart, we are still emotionally tied by the fear and trauma that I am going through right now.

What were the trappings? Shame: Shame that I wasn't worth changing for. Why couldn't he love me enough to want to change? Guilt: I lied many times to cover for his behavior. I still struggle with guilt for not getting my children out sooner. Fear: Fear of the unknown. As horrible as my life was with Steve, what would it be like without him? Where would we go? What would he do to me if he found me? Financial: I had no extra money to rent an apartment. I wouldn't have a car. How would I get to work? Sanctity of marriage: I believed in my wedding vows, but this is not what we promised each other either. His threats: Steve often told me that if he couldn't have me, no one could! He would kill me first. He told me that if I ever left him, he would tell my parents about the abortion. Then they would know that their sweet, little daughter was really a monster. (He never did tell them. Just as his promises were empty, so were some of his threats.) Looking back, I showed strength by staying. But even more, when realizing that it was never going to get better and was, in fact, spiraling down, I showed more strength by saying, "Enough!" Leaving my abusive marriage behind me, staying away, and not giving in to the fear of retaliation took more courage than I thought I possessed but I know now that God was my backbone.

My goal for this week is: I am going to focus on the things said to me now and will not allow the things he said to me over eleven years ago still affect me.

What is trapping you? Is it shame? Guilt? Fear? Devotion? Responsibilities? Do you believe the awful things he says to you? God wants to bring you into a spacious place—a place where you have the freedom to know real love, to rest, and feel safe.

He reached down from on high and took hold of me; he drew me out of deep waters. He rescued me from my powerful enemy, from my foes, who were too strong for me. They confronted me in the day of my disaster, but the Lord was my support. He brought me out into a spacious place; he rescued me because he delighted in me. (Psalm 18:16-19)

February 17

Last night I had an interesting dream. Steve and I were sorting through things because we were splitting up and deciding who should take what. We were looking at some pictures of the truck Steve drove when we were together. He seemed so sad looking at them. I edged toward him and gave him a hug. He felt like a little boy. I felt tremendous empathy for him, but that did not change that I was leaving him.

> I saw him sitting there so very small,
> I almost didn't know who he was.
> For when I knew him long ago
> He didn't look quite so lost.
>
> He was huge, with energy that had no direction
> Except to hate and hurt along the way.
> He shadowed over all my hopes and dreams,
> He stole the light from my day.
>
> How did he become such a small child?
> When did he become so defenseless and afraid?
> Could it be he never was all that I saw?
> Could it be he never was that brave?

Steve has always been this bigger-than-life person to me. He's finally shrinking down to real size, and he's not brave and strong. I'm finally seeing him as he really is.

February 25

I hurt. My heart hurts. My emotions are infected and bleeding, but I can't admit to my fragile condition. Nobody knows my anguish. I try to keep it all surrounded in humor. Nobody knows. Sometimes it's all I can do to go to work and then home again. It's all I can do to go to Bible study or to meet with friends. I want to hide. Something in me is locked up. I just can't do life like this anymore, and then I feel guilty and ashamed for not being there for others. I simply have nothing to give right now. Nobody knows . . . but God.

March 13

My heart is waking up. I'm more aware of feelings or at least I'm realizing that it's OK to have them and that it's safe for me to feel. And I'm starting to realize more than ever that I would like to be married. I feel as if I could trust a man again. The thing is, I want to be married, but I don't want to go through the dating process. I'm just so bad at dating! When I told Dane about my new feelings, and how surprised I am by the depth of my desire and the depth of my sadness that I'm alone, he was happy for me! Those feelings are so far on the other side of where I was six months ago. I told him I was glad he was so pleased with my misery!

We talked about my being in such a hurry to hit the goal, in other words, be married without dating. He told me of a book called "Deadline" by Randy Alcorn. Apparently a man goes to heaven thinking he didn't have to do anything once he was there. He had reached his goal, but Jesus told him that there are goals in heaven too. We have to learn that there is joy in the process of reaching the goal; we need to enjoy the process. That hit home with me. Little Miss Chart-Your-Progress lady. Enjoy the process! I miss out on a lot because I can only think of the goal.

I asked Dane if it might be time to cancel our visits. He told me that if I was gauging my need to see him based on my functionality, I wouldn't need to come—I am functioning fine. To be honest, I can see big improvements. I feel like parts of me are waking up. Some of it feels good but some of it . . . and then there is that one thing that we still have not talked about.

March 15

Last night I dreamed again that Steve and I were together. We were getting along OK. We were going out to the garage to practice with the band. In the doorway I told him this was the last time I would play. It was time to make some changes. I told him we could play around campfires and such but no more bars. He asked me if I was turning into duds like my parents. I asked him why their lifestyle is so awful—maybe he should take a look at it. They're happy and at peace with life. He should look at his own parents—always fighting and surrounded with some sort of conflict. He looked at me as if he had never put that together. We went on to practice but the whole time I was worried about afterward when everyone left. Would he beat me up?

March 20

My visit with Dane was exhausting. We talked about things that I'm afraid of when I think about being in a relationship. Honesty is important to me but that involves opening up to a man, and that's very hard for me.

We talked about trusting and allowing myself to be vulnerable to a man. What was my heart saying? I sobbed. My hands went to my mouth. It was almost like I was trying to push the words back in but they came out. Slowly. Sometimes too quietly. For me, love has consisted of hurt, lies, shame, humiliation, worthlessness, smashed hopes, fear, pain, hiding. You do not share emotions, feelings, or thoughts because they are stupid. Because it gets him riled up. Because he throws it in your face. Because he makes a joke out of them to others—so you hold them inside. You start to believe it isn't important how you feel anyway. Smashed hopes. You go into a marriage loving and feeling loved. You're certain that it's forever. To be loved is empowering, and you have great dreams. Each time I was beaten, a hope was smashed. Afterward he would promise me it would not happen again, and I would believe him until he would beat me again and then another hope was smashed. I felt worthless because I was told I was.

Steve had countless affairs and enjoyed bragging about them. He never hesitated to parade them in front of me. They would either be "friends" or people I knew too. He would be very graphic about what they did together. He thought if he told me about it, somehow it made it OK. Sometimes when we had sex, he would tell me I didn't do it as well as so-and-so. If I cried, I'd get hit. If I showed disinterest, I'd get hit. No matter what, I got hit. He beat me with words, with fists, and with his abusive sex.

I quit talking except to my kids. I didn't care about anything except my children. When people were around I put on a show; on the inside, I was humiliated and insulted by his behavior, but it seemed better to act like I didn't care. Just stuff those feelings.

Telling Dane about what happened was frightening because when I said it outloud, I was acknowledging that it really did occur. I have to tell myself that I am safe now. Steve CANNOT hurt me.

Can you freely express how you feel? Do you stuff your feelings inside for fear of ridicule? Do you find yourself pretending because it is the safer thing to do? Tell God how you really feel about your day, your week, your life.

In my distress I called to the Lord; I called out to my God. From his temple he heard my voice; my cry came to his ears.
(2 Samuel 22:7)

March 23

It has only been three days since I saw Dane, but I am back again. We both got to his office at the same time. He went in to turn on the lights as I paced in the waiting room. Tears were already flowing. It was going to be a wet hour! He asked me what was going on. I told him about my Tuesday after I left our session. I almost called work and told them I wouldn't be in. I didn't think I could pull myself together. But I didn't call in nor did I pull myself together. I took a 1½-hour lunch. Me, the person who usually eats at her desk. I went to the nearest grocery store and bought a pile of junk food, went to the park and gorged myself. I went back to work feeling horrible so left work early. I got home and under grandma's quilt I ate and ate, slept and ate some more.

On Wednesday I went to work and at lunchtime went to one of my favorite shops. I love going there because the shop is full of pretty things. It smells good and they play wonderful music. It is a good place to get lost. The theme from "Somewhere in Time" began playing and I had instant tears, more like sobs. Where did that come from? I had to get out of there.

I have to get out of this stuck place. What is happening to me? I seem to be in self-destruct mode. I feel like I'm out hanging in the middle of nothing—like all the stuffing is being pulled out of me. Knowing, in my mind, what has happened is one thing; but when you say it outloud it becomes so ugly—so vile. It was all so long ago. Why can't I just leave it there? I look at all of the ways I have been blessed, but I'm stuck.

How do I move on after these sessions? I need to learn some survival tactics. Dane said that first we have to understand what's going on. I told him that even though he thinks I don't really trust him, I must—more than others because I have let him pull out some of my stuffing.

We talked about my gorging. He said that when a person feels "poured out," as I did after that last session, one often feels the need to "fill up" again, be it drugs, food, alcohol, shopping, or sex. In my case it was food. Amazingly, what we fill up on can be harmful, so we need to determine a healthier way to do this. "Now," Dane said, "what are you going to do for yourself today? What are you going to do to fill yourself up?" I couldn't answer him at that moment but I knew it was something I had to work on.

Dane reminded me that Jesus never intended for us to be alone. He said I needed garden friends. When Christ went into the Garden of Gethsemane to pray, He needed to surround Himself with friends—"Garden Friends." This means I would have to reach out—something that's excruciatingly hard for me—trusting, being vulnerable, and trusting some more.

Do you ever feel "poured out"? Make a list of what you do to fill yourself back up. Do you need to make some changes?

May the God of hope fill you with all joy and peace as you trust in him, so that you may overflow with hope by the power of the Holy Spirit. (Romans 15:13)

March 26

Dane suggested that I read "Redeeming Love" by Francine Rivers. I had read it once before but the first time I read it, I felt annoyed at Angel for not being content. Sure, she had a rough start and some awful things happened to her, but now—now she had a husband who loved her and loved God. He would take care of her; he would look beyond her past. She was beautiful. Get over it, Angel, get your act together, and enjoy being rescued.

This time when I read it, I felt great compassion toward Angel. In spite of the wonderful life she had now, she couldn't shake who she had been and what had happened to her. She couldn't forgive herself. She didn't feel worthy of anything good. She constantly wanted to go back to the familiar, even though she hated it. She didn't feel worthy of Michael's love and certainly not of God's. It was important for me to read "Redeeming Love" because it showed me how powerful the mind can be. It won't allow good things to happen because we are convinced that we are unworthy. The wall we build to protect ourselves also blocks things out. Like love.

Slowly he peeled away at the walls
She had worked so hard to build.
She held back, afraid of the echoed call
In the memories the inner wall held.

He wanted to open the door to a life
Of freedom to be loved and to feel.
She only knew a love stabbed with strife
Yet she waited for him as he peeled.

Sometimes the peeling brought him near
To things she wasn't ready to see.
But quietly he'd wait as she fought the fear—
Watching her struggle to finally be free.

He knew in time the peeling would end
And with confidence she could face her fear.
She'd finally look beyond what had happened
And in God's love she would feel secure.

What are your walls made of? Are they tough and hard so that no one can break through and hurt you anymore? Are you afraid to love? What is real love anyway?

Love is patient, love is kind. It does not envy, it does not boast, it is not proud. It is not rude, it is not self-seeking, it is not easily angered, it keeps no record of wrong doings. Love does not delight in evil but rejoices with the truth. It always protects, always trusts, always hopes, always perseveres. (1 Corinthians 13:4-7)

April 10

Dane is concerned that I no longer watch/listen/read the news or weather. I have no interest. He asked how long this had been going on. I told him I thought several weeks. It is not as if I woke up one day and made a conscious decision to avoid the outside world. He told me that when we cannot control what is going on inside of us we try to control what is outside. I do it by avoiding—just as I have done with what is buried deep inside of me. But now it is time to face that too.

Tiny baby held gently in His arms
Quietly wondering why you were the one.
Know, my sweet child, you were saved from life's
harms
Yet I shouldn't have let you go, my son.

No matter how much I justify
The choice I made long ago,
I can only answer my heart cry—
So afraid, and too weak to say no.

Sweet child, I still think of you each day,
I wonder how you would have grown.
If only God's word I'd obeyed,
I was wrong, I should have known.

But this, my son, is what I want to say,
I am so sorry and my heart is of love—
Wanting to hold you as I should have that day
Yet know I will in heaven above.

Before we moved to our duplex, our life together was a mess.
Steve wouldn't hold down a job—he wanted to party. He was
running around with a crowd I didn't like. His friends were
more important than the kids and me. There were so many
beatings and so many girlfriends, too many trips to the
welfare office, too many nights lying in bed alone, wondering
who he was with this time.

I left Steve a couple of times but this time I had the courage to tell him I was not coming back until he got a job and I saw the first paycheck. I thought if he was working, he would feel better about himself and behave. He found a job in another town and eventually we moved there. It was an exciting time. Steve worked hard and was acting like a husband and father. When both of the kids were in school, I went to work too. We bought a duplex and Steve worked hard to fix it up. Then I got pregnant even though I was using birth control. Steve was livid. He screamed at me that I was finally skinny and now I was going to get fat and ugly again. He told me if I had this baby, I would have three kids to raise alone. He ranted about the boat he wanted. If I had this baby, he wouldn't be able to buy that stupid boat. The violence started up again. The memory of him hitting me on the side of my pregnant stomach haunted me.

Now I was pregnant again and so afraid life would go back to what it had been—beatings, cheating, partying, welfare—all of it. Steve wanted me to have an abortion; it was an ugly choice I never thought I would have to face. It was inconceivable. We fought and we fought and at the end, I gave in. I hated him for forcing me to have the abortion, but I hated myself more for giving in. Where were the spunk and the fight? Where was my faith? Was I so beaten down, so afraid, feeling so worthless that I couldn't be what I believed in? I felt so ashamed.

First we had to go to the clinic for a consultation with a therapist, and later I went for the abortion. I remember staring out the car window the entire way. The waiting room was full of women of all ages. I looked around and wondered—are you the one waiting or the one doing this horrible thing? A girl sat across from us, a larger girl in bib overalls, who couldn't stop crying. She was all alone.

My turn came to go into the procedure room. I got up on the bed and put my feet in the stirrups. A nurse started chatting with me about all sorts of things. I think her job was to distract me. The doctor started the vacuum. I thought, "Change your mind—don't do it," but I was too scared. Steve would explode. I would have to ride home with him fuming. During the procedure, I remember the nurse stopped talking and made a strange face. I asked her what was wrong, and she replied everything was OK, but I still wonder if my baby was alive.

Next was the recovery room. It was long and narrow, lined with recliners and a door in the middle. No one made eye contact as people came in. It was as if everyone was ashamed. A young girl with long, blond hair reclined next to me, shivering. I asked her if she needed a blanket and asked the nurse to get her one. Then I sat and waited. I just wanted to leave.

On the way down to the parking lot, Steve held me in the elevator. He kept saying we did the right thing. I was stone. I did not respond. I felt nothing but disgust toward him and myself, and forever trapped by the hideous thing I had done.

I wanted to go to Target afterward to buy something for the kids. When we got into the store, Steve went a different direction. I found something for the kids, and I bought a needlepoint picture to work on.

When we got home, I was feeling tired, shaky, and very, very sad. But Steve said, "It's done, it's over with, and there won't be anymore crying about it." That night as I lay on the floor watching TV, I felt shame and sadness choking me. I couldn't stop crying. I told Steve I was cramping when the truth was—inside I was dying. Steve went in to the kitchen to get me a glass of water and just stood at the sink staring out the window. He had no idea what to do.

I started working on the needlepoint. I was obsessed with it. I did my own color schemes. It was beautiful. I worked on it all of the time. Every moment. My world was my needlepoint and my kids. I shut out other family and friends. I wanted nothing to do with Steve. He would try to hug me, but I was like a cement block. I didn't want him near me. He told me the abortion was over with, and it was for the best. He didn't want me moping around feeling sorry for myself. Each time he said it, I froze up a little more. When I finished my beautiful picture, I held it for a few minutes and then threw it away. It represented deep, ugly shame.

After a while Steve became frustrated with me. He started drinking and going out more, but I didn't care. I simply did not care. I had become a fake. Pretend I care, pretend I don't care. Pretend it's all OK, pretend it doesn't matter.

I felt that I didn't have the right to mourn or to even wonder what my baby would have been like. What would his voice sound like? What would he look like? Would he be funny or serious? When you miscarry, people comfort you. When you abort, you feel alone. You made the choice, the ugly decision to end that life. You haven't earned the right or the privilege to mourn the loss because you did it.

Have you had an abortion? Is there something else that is draining joy from your life. You need to tell God right now. It is his forgiveness that will permit your life to fill with joy again. When God forgives, he forgets!

He will not always accuse, nor will he harbor his anger forever; he does not treat us as our sins deserve or repay us according to our iniquities . . . as far as the east is from the west, so far has he removed our transgressions from us. (Psalm 103:9-10,12)

May 9

I read the book "Trying to Measure Up" by Jeff Van Vonderen. Before I even bought the book I had this thought: why do I feel like I don't deserve to be loved unless I have earned it? How could anyone love me unless I did something for them and love was my reward? I'm so glad it isn't that way with God. He loves me—with no conditions—and that will never, ever change.

May 12

My visit with Dane emptied me. I told him I don't know "me" anymore. I was always the one who had plans every night of the week. Now when friends call, I either don't return their calls or I lie and say I'm already busy. My house is a mess. I have laundry to fold from last week. My suitcase still has stuff in it from my New York trip over a week ago. I finally went through three weeks of mail. My finances are a mess. The inside of my car looks like a dump truck. I poured out milk that had an expiration dated two months ago; it had never been opened.

My office has piles lying everywhere. This isn't me, and yet it bothers me that it doesn't bother me enough to change it. I am weary of the battle. What is going on? Depression. I've had to fight hard to survive, and now I can finally allow the sadness, the hurt, the anger, the helplessness, and the fear to come out. Now I can do it. I can do it because I am safe. My heart is truly catching up to my mind.

Once again Dane brought up my childhood. I'm so tired of this! Why is he not listening to me? I was safe as a child. I was extremely naive. I felt too responsible for other people's happiness and was too softhearted. Had I had more experience in dating or even being around guys, maybe I would have seen signs. I was very trusting because I had no reason not to be. Dane goes on and on about it like he wants to blame all of it on my past. What makes me so angry is that he's not listening to me. I told him how I was feeling, and he laughed! Can you believe it? He said I was funny. I was furious! How dare he laugh at my feelings! He thought my explanation was canned, rehearsed, and that I was being flippant. My blood was boiling when I left.

I tried to explain just how I felt
When we talked about my past.
A shy, unsure child I was—
Some feelings last and last;
And he laughed at me.

I told him my frustrations.
I think that he is wrong
To take me down a path
Where I simply don't belong;
And he laughed at me.

He knows how I tremble
How I feel insecure
To go against what a man says
Or to let a man near—
And he laughed at me.

He said I am funny.
Did what I say even matter?
I felt insignificant,
I feel even sadder
Because he laughed at me.

May 30

I went back to Dane, and we talked about the poem and the feelings behind it. He apologized. I learned something; there is risk in confrontation but it doesn't have to be the end of a relationship. You can move on if you want to. I also learned this—I can do it! I can disagree with a man and let him know it. Along with my heart waking up, I am becoming more confident. I was able to stand up to Dane for what I believed. Man, did that feel good!

July 7

I am feeling ready. I am ready to love again. I am ready to be loved. I am ready to trust. Will I be perfect at this? Probably not but I want to try. I want to share my life with this elusive guy who doesn't have a face yet, but I pray for him. I wonder how God will bring us together.

Somewhere out there he looks at the moon
And prays he will soon meet me.
He wonders if God will let it happen soon,
And reminds himself to wait patiently.

Somewhere out there he wants to share
His life and his love with me.
He knows that God truly cares
So he waits for me quietly.

Somewhere out there he cries in the night
Wondering how he can bear it alone.
Tired of the echoes in his life and the fight
Of being on his own.

Please wait for me, it won't be much longer.
I still have some things I must do.
I am learning to trust and let go of the fear,
And when I'm ready, God will bring me to you.

August 15

I have seen Dane for the last time. I'm going to miss him. As frustrated as I got with him at times, he gently led me through this dark time in my life. He prayed with me, cried with me, and laughed with me. He helped me to understand at my own pace. I thank God for him.

The ship quietly left the harbor
Where it rested during the storm.
With the anchor pulled up and sails to the wind,
Once again it had been saved from harm.

The constant waves gently rocked the ship
As it sailed on its new course.
Not sure of where it was heading
But aware of the wind's gentle force.

Sometimes the night water grew choppy,
But the ship found the strength to press on.
It knew if the storm grew stronger
It could rest in the harbor 'til dawn.

And then again the ship would set sail
With the harbor not too far behind
To venture into new waters
While the harbor stayed close in mind.

Good-bye Dane.

If you journaled through this part of the book, I hope you have realized you are not alone; God is listening to you and through His word, He is talking to you too! Your tears can bring joy because God delights in you and wants to rescue you. He wants to fill you with joy and peace. He is waiting to forgive you. All you have to do is ask to be His child. You were born into a family on earth. Now, be "born again" into God's family.

In reply Jesus declared, "I tell you the truth, no one can see the kingdom of God unless he is born again." (John 3:3)

Filled with Hope

With the exception of one visit, it has been 1½ years since I have seen Dane. If I were to give you one word that has carried me, it is PROMISE. Isn't that almost funny? I lived for 19 years on empty promises. As each promise was broken, so was another thread of trust. Yet I am fully able to believe in promises again because they are made by someone who has been faithful to me all along—Jesus.

Right, you say. Where was God during the beatings? Where was He when I was being choked? Where was He when I walked into that abortion clinic? This was really hard for me to understand. A year ago I started a Bible study because I wanted answers. Now that I am learning just how much God loves me, it is hard for me to fully understand how He could allow all those things to happen.

I asked Jesus into my heart when I was eight years old, so I was His child for a very long time. Along the way, though, I made some choices that were not what God would have wanted for me, and the consequences of those choices were horrible. God has made His "rules" not to cramp our style, not to take the fun out of life. He made them to protect us. He knows what is going to hurt us. He knows how it will affect our lives. God was with me all along, but I chose to look the other way. He hadn't gone anywhere.

The memories can still make me tremble. As I write some of this, I am sitting here under my grandma's quilt with my Bible on my lap. The Bible is where all the promises come from. I would like to share a few of them with you.

He tells me that He has seen my sinful ways but He will heal me, guide me, and restore comfort to me. (There is hope after abortion!) (Isaiah 57:18)

He tells me that though I'd seen troubles, many and bitter, He will restore my life again (that's my second chance!). From the depths of the earth, He will again bring me up. He will increase my honor and comfort me again.
(Psalm 71:20)

He tells me that He goes before me and will be with me. He will not leave me nor forsake me. I should not be afraid or discouraged. (Courage to write this book!) (Deuteronomy 31:16)

He tells me that everyone who calls on the name of the Lord will be saved. (Romans 10:13)

He tells me that He will hold my right hand and say to me, "Fear not, I will help you." (Isaiah 41:13) Isn't that much better than junk food aisle 7 at the grocery store?

He tells me that He has swept away my offenses like a cloud, my sins like the morning mist. He tells me to return to Him for He has redeemed me. (Isaiah 44:22) Isn't that a wonderful promise? God will not throw my mistakes in my face. He won't use my mistakes as an excuse to hurt me. He has swept away my sins like the morning mist. THEY ARE NO MORE because I am His child.

He tells me that He reached down from on high and took hold of me. He drew me out of deep waters. He rescued me from my powerful enemy, from my foes who were too strong for me. They confronted me in my day of disaster but the Lord was my support. He brought me into a spacious place (I am no longer trapped!). He rescued me because He delights in me!! (Psalm 18:17)

Our Heavenly Father wants to save you because He delights in you too! It does not matter what you have done. It does not matter what has been done to you. If you are His child, He has a book full of promises for you. He keeps His promises. They are not empty words. He won't leave you. He won't beat you. All you have to do is ask Him to be your Heavenly Father, your Savior. He is simply waiting for your invitation.

I came back to Him after so many years
What could I possibly say?
Down on my knees with hands held in front
I had forgotten how to pray.

But as the tears came, I felt Him near.
It was then that I knew for sure.
God heard me pray even without words,
For I simply was the prayer.

I came back to Him though He never left me,
As I moved from sin to sin.
He kept talking to me but I would not hear,
I would not let Him in.

And then one day when I could take no more,
From God I could no longer hide—
I knew at last I had found the Hope
That had never left my side.

Now on God's book of promises
My new life is being built.
With His hope, love, and happiness,
I'm peeking out from "Under Grandma's Quilt".

It's hard to understand His love. He loves you no matter what—even if you have had an abortion. Even if terrible things were done to you and you are convinced that no one could ever love you again. In fact, He loves you so much that He sent His only Son, Jesus, to die on the cross. His death gave you two things—forgiveness because our sins died with Jesus, and eternal life because Jesus came back to life three days later. That gift will bring you to heaven when you die. Jesus tells us in John 5:24 *"I tell you the truth, whoever hears my word and believes him who sent me has eternal life and will not be condemned; he has crossed over from death to life."* Another one of His wonderful promises!

Why not invite Him now? Just pray these words. Dear Jesus, whatever I have done, whatever has been done to me, I know that you love me. I believe what you have promised in the Bible. I ask you to take away my sins and be a part of my life forever. Amen.

> Once I was covered with confusion and fear
> A shroud of pain heavily draped over me.
> It discouraged everyone from coming too near—
> I was hiding yet wanting to be free.
>
> But a soft light came from deep inside
> And gently pushed its way to my heart.
> For the first time I felt the need to confide,
> And with Christ I knew I could start.
>
> I wonder as the soft light slowly breaks through
> How God can still love and care for me.
> Yet His soft light reflects only what is true
> And casts no shadows while it helps me see.
>
> My Savior is tenderly drawing me
> To the place where the soft light shines.
> Where I'll no longer hide behind my story,
> For now I am His and He is mine.

God's love has been my lamp. His lamp lights each step as I go through life. It lights just enough so I can take one step at a time. Anymore and I would be overwhelmed.

The soft light is Jesus' love. It is not a bright, glowing light—that would be too harsh, too blinding. Instead it's a warm, inviting, gentle light. It allows me to see just what I need to see at this moment. God is my lamp. Jesus is my light.

Now I can almost always talk about the abuse without crying. But anytime I talk about my children and what they saw and heard, the fear they must have felt, the confusion, the disgust, it is still very hard. They deserved a childhood like mine, safe and full of love. Yet they have grown into wonderful, loving, talented, and very funny adults who have brought me to the lighter side of life. There is no doubt in my mind but that God has given me an extra blessing here!!

I do not carry many of my yesterdays inside anymore. I feel sad for things that I did, and I feel sad for what my children saw. I no longer hate Steve for what he did to us. Somehow, and I know it can only be because of Jesus, I have forgiven him—and no one is more surprised by that than I. There was a time I did not want to forgive Steve. To me that was condoning what he did. It let him off the hook. I wanted him to suffer as I had—as my children had. The impact of his behavior has tentacles that still reach into parts of my life, but it no longer controls any part of it. God has taken what certainly could have crippled me and instead changed me.

Do you know, I can now enjoy remembering and talking about some of the sweeter times of our marriage . . . fishing trips, holidays, moving into our home on the lake, watching our children grow, boat parades on the 4th of July, our crazy dog stories, some of my life-threatening cooking mishaps! I can even look at some of my "band days" with a chuckle. All those times were a part of my life too. Forgiving Steve broke the chains to the dark side of my past and has allowed me to move on with a smile.

Does this mean I trust Steve? No. But I do trust God. I trust Him to continue to protect me. He has also given me discernment, and I am not going to put myself in situations that are threatening. God has given you and me this wonderful promise in Jeremiah 29:11. *"For I know the plans I have for you," declares the Lord, "plans to prosper you and not to harm you, plans to give you hope and a future."* Please—let Him keep that promise for you too.

Do I still spend time under grandma's quilt? Yes, it has become more thread bare, more seams are separating, but it's still holding together—a lot like me! And I spend time under it for different reasons now. Give me a fragrant cup of coffee, a lighted candle, soft music, a good book, and my grandma's quilt. I am settled for the evening. The night that Steve beat me in the van, he asked me what I wanted out of life. I told him my children and peace. I finally have it.

"He will cover you with his feathers, and under his wings you will find refuge; his faithfulness will be your shield and rampart." (Psalm 91:4)

Afterthoughts

Dear Friends,

If reading this book has brought you hope or understanding, then it has done what was intended. Writing this was both joy-filled and sometimes very hard. I couldn't have done it without my "Garden Friends." Family and friends encouraged me and helped me with everything from computers to funding this book to praying for me. To each of you, I thank you.

One of the hardest times during all of this was losing Dane. On a beautiful summer morning, Dane collapsed while jogging and died. He started as my psychologist and eleven months later, I considered him an incredible friend. Now he was gone. I was almost done with my book and was excited to tell him about it, but I never had a chance. He was a man who loved God, his family, and life. I will always be grateful for him and will never forget how much he helped me.

To my mom and dad, brothers and sisters—please do not feel guilty for not coming to my rescue. How could you? You did not know. I worked very hard at covering all of the ugliness. I stayed away when times were at their worst. I became an incredible actress in order to survive. If you would've stepped in, I probably would have defended Steve. That is how confused I was. Had you stepped in, Steve would have punished me. When I finally reached out and let you know I was in trouble—that is when I needed you the most. Every one of you was there for Natalie, Tony, and me. You helped me move, you helped me financially, you helped me feed my children, you were willing to come to my home when I was the most afraid. And to this day, you have never stopped praying for us. You did everything just right!

To my sisters, you let me cry, and you made me laugh—always exactly when I needed it. You were my anchors with a tissue. Thank you!

To my brothers, you cared and you encouraged and you provided great knowledge. Thank you!

To my mom and dad, you heard me cry, you held me up, you believed in me, you understood. Thank you!

To my daughter-in-law, son-in-law, and my grandchildren, thank you to each of you for loving me. I love you too.

And to my children . . .

You move quietly in the wind but you're never far from sight;
Against blue skies you freely roam.
You brought me smiles even when life wasn't right—
Wherever you are, to me, is home.

You are the balloons of my life, you made me stand tall,
Even when I hung my head in shame.
Your love held me up when I wanted to fall;
You gave me love and took away blame.

I gave you life; you gave me a reason to live.
My love for you continues to deepen.
You are the balloons of my heart, filled up with love.
God blessed me with you as my children.

To my new friends, I would love to hear from you. If you want to tell me what is on your mind, please write me at:

RHO
PO Box 131875
St. Paul, MN 55113-0021

If it is safe for me to reply, let me know the address to write you back. I would be honored. Remember, you are loved, you are special, you do have hope, and God delights in you!

Under His wings,

Rho

Every day I am aware of how far God has brought me and how grateful I am. Because of this, my desire is for all battered women to know that there is great hope! And for all post-abortion women—there is sweet forgiveness. If this little book has blessed you or blessed someone that you care about and you want to be part of spreading this hope, I would be grateful for your prayer and financial support. This book has been meant to be free to battered women. Your gifts will make this happen.

RHO
PO Box 131875
St. Paul, MN 55113-0021

The purpose of "Under Grandma's Quilt" is to open the eyes of those not exposed to abuse and/or abortion and share the tears and the victories of those who live it. I would love to visit your group and share my story. If you are looking for a speaker, please write to the above address. I look forward to meeting you!

Thank you for caring,

Rho

Telephone Numbers

Abortion   Caring Pregnancy Center   1-800-395-HELP (4357)
Call if you are considering abortion or have had one.

Abuse   If emergency, call 911

National Domestic Violence Hotline 1-800-799-SAFE (7233)
Call to find options of where to go and how you can be helped
through programs in your area.

National Victim Center   1-800-FYI-CALL (394-2255)
Options available are: Advocate for victims, Attorney referrals
They provide legal information rather than counseling
Web site: www.ncvc.com

Counseling/Spiritual

Focus on the Family   1-719-531-3400 x2700
You can call and leave your phone number. A licensed counselor
or ordained chaplain will contact you. Focus on the Family has an
excellent Web site that covers many topics. It is easy to use—try
it! www.troubledwith.com

Safety Plan

Please use this at your discretion. These are good things to think about but if your abuser has any indication that you are doing this, you could put yourself in danger.

This plan is an abbreviated version of one provided by the Pennsylvania Coalition against Domestic Violence. Contact your State Coalition for a more detailed plan but this will give you a basic idea of what you should think about if you are still in an unsafe environment.

1. You cannot always avoid violent incidents. To increase your safety, you can use a variety of strategies.

   A. Practice getting out safely if there is an emergency. What doors, windows, elevators can you use? Teach them to your children.

   B. Teach your children to call 911.

   C. Teach your children to flee the house or hide during a violent situation. Instruct them to NEVER try to break up a violent incident.

   D. Keep your purse and car keys or copies of them in a specific place so that if you must leave quickly, you can.

E. Tell trusted people that if they should hear suspicious noises or a certain signal (such as a porch light on during the day) that they should call the police.

F. Use a code word as a signal to your children or a friend that they should call for help.

G. Try to avoid arguments in the bathroom, garage, kitchen, near weapons, or in rooms without an outside exit.

H. During an attack, try to wrap your arms around your head to protect it and curl up to protect your stomach. Do not verbally defend yourself or argue with him during a beating. He is irrational, and he may become more violent. If you can act in self-defense (hit, run, scream for help because it is nearby) to save further injury, do it. After an attack, see a doctor to assess the injuries. You could be more severely hurt than you realize. It is important that this assault be reported to the police.

2. When preparing to leave your husband, you should plan your departure. Do not tell him you are leaving. Leave when he is out or tell him you are going to run an errand.

   A. Decide with whom or where outside of the home you will leave the following items: money, an extra set of car and house keys, clothes for the children and yourself. If you do not have a car, decide what bus or train you could take or if you could borrow a car.

   B. Decide where you would go. A friend's home may work if you have their permission and your abuser will not find you there, or find out about a shelter nearby. I must remind you—if you plan on going to a friend's or nearby family's home, you could put them in danger. When possible, a shelter for battered women is your best choice.

   C. Decide where to hide important documents that you can quickly grab when you flee.

   D. Have a list of telephone numbers with you, such as the numbers listed in this book, local police station, children's school, minister.

   E. Open a savings account. Every penny adds up.

Take the time to think about all of the things you may need if you should have to quickly flee. Have a plan in mind. We are bright women, and we can be very resourceful when necessary. Do not doubt that.

*The Lord himself goes before you
and will be with you, he will
never leave you nor forsake you.
Do not be afraid, do not be
discouraged.*
(Deuteronomy 31:8)